INTERACTIVE BULLETIN BOARDS AS TEACHING TOOLS

Joan M. Dungey

nea PROFESSIONAL LIBRARY
National Education Association
Washington, D.C.

ACKNOWLEDGMENT

The author wishes to thank the following educators for their assistance in preparing this publication: Janet Brokenbek, Plainview, Texas; Elaine Brouwer, Seattle, Washington; and Janeta Fong, Kearney, Nebraska.

Printing History
  First Printing: May 1989

Note

The opinions expressed in this publication shold not be construed as representing the policy or position of the National Education Association. Materials published by the NEA Professional Library are intended to be discussion documents for educators who are concerned with specialized interests of the profession.

Library-of-Congress Cataloging-in-Publication Data

Dungey, Joan M.
    Interactive bulletin boards as teaching tools/ Joan M. Dungey.
        P.   cm. — (Analysis and action series)
    Bibliography: p.
    ISBN 0-8106-3340-X
    1. Bulletin boards.   2. Teaching—Aids and devices.   I. Title.
II. Series.
LB1043.58.D86   1989
371.3'356-dc19   89-3014
                                                         CIP

CONTENTS

Preface 5

Chapter 1. Bulletin Boards and the Classroom 6
  Helping the Student... 6
  Helping the Teacher... 7

Chapter 2. Uses of Bulletin Boards 11
  Announce 11
  Beautify.. 11
  Display... 12
  Demonstrate 12
  Share 13
  Instruct.. 13

Chapter 3. Review of the Literature 15
  Research Studies... 15
  Discussion of Research 17

Chapter 4. Level I: Display Bulletin Boards............................. 20
  Guidelines... 20
  Procedures... 21
  Examples 25

Chapter 5. Level II: Discussion Bulletin Boards 27
  Procedures... 27
  Examples 30

Chapter 6. Level III: Interactive Bulletin Boards 32
  Procedures... 32
  Examples 36

Chapter 7. Level IV: Student-Made Bulletin Boards 40
  Guidelines... 40

Chapter 8. A Practical Application: Bulletin Board Maps
Across the Curriculum 43
  Premapping 47
  Interdisciplinary Maps.. 47
  Reading/Language Arts... 50
  Social Studies 53
  Mathematics 60
  Science 66
  Other Activities.. 74

Bibliography 79

The Author

Joan M. Dungey, a fourth grade teacher at Hillel Academy, Dayton, Ohio, has taught at all grade levels, both elementary and secondary. She is the author of numerous articles for professional journals, as well as a book, and presents seminars on interactive bulletin boards to teachers across the country.

The Advisory Panel

Dave Bird, Instructor in Writing/E.S.L., Leeward Community College, Pearl City, Hawaii

Nancy Tyler Demartra, Teacher, Louisville, Kentucky

Thomas W. Hine, Jr., Sixth Grade Teacher, Henry A. Wolcott School, West Hartford, Connecticut

Cricket Kelley, Language Arts Teacher, J. T. Reddick Middle School, Tifton, Georgia

Stanley M. Lucas, Mathematics Instructor, Extension Division, University of Florida, Gainesville

Ann Mobbs, Library Director, Wallace Community College, Selma, Alabama

Karen L. Washington, English Teacher, Jennings High School, Jennings, Missouri

Jeanne Stenson Whitesell, Second Grade Teacher, Gibbs International Studies Magnet School, Little Rock, Arkansas

PREFACE

What is your first impression upon entering a building, a house, or a classroom? If you will be spending a great deal of time there, you expect a comfortable feeling of belonging. Its decor should match its purpose. In an office building, you expect to see working equipment, a businesslike atmosphere. In a home, you expect warmth, a sense of welcome or friendship, each room filled with the "tools of homemaking"—the appropriate furniture and appliances. Like a home, a classroom needs welcoming warmth and a comfortable atmosphere to promote the risk-taking that learning entails. You expect to see student desks, teacher's desk, pens, pencils, books, paper, chalkboards. But there should be more: color, welcoming announcements, and walls covered with eye-catching, mind-catching ideas, beckoning you the moment you enter, reaching out to envelop you in curiosity. A classroom of bare walls or chalkboards limits students' natural curiosity and interest.

Bulletin boards can help achieve this sense of belonging, this cooperative spirit, this excitement about learning. What should welcoming bulletin boards contain? Certainly some color and perhaps a greeting, but also a glimpse into the learning topics to come to stimulate students' interest. Teachers want students to be "buzzing" when they enter the classroom: about what they see, about what they think will be taught—learning already and thinking about learning.

A classroom should also be a place of refuge and security, where students are not ridiculed or put down and are free to express their emotions as well as their curiosity. Interactive bulletin boards allow students to express their individuality in a nonthreatening atmosphere. They are usually open-ended, noncompetitive, and have no time limitations.

This publication shows how to plan for bulletin boards that will achieve these ends for both teachers and students. It reports the research and gives detailed instructions for making four different levels of bulletin boards: display, discussion, interactive, and student-made. It also includes suggestions for creating specific bulletin boards, and for using one concept—mapping—across all content areas and in all grades.

Chapter 1

BULLETIN BOARDS
AND THE CLASSROOM

Classrooms exist for students; their purpose is to educate students. Therefore, anything teachers do or use in the classroom must relate to helping students learn; bulletin boards are no exception.

HELPING THE STUDENT

Bulletin boards that instruct relate to topics that students are studying; they contribute aesthetically to the classroom, making for a comfortable learning atmosphere. They add to a lesson, reviewing, reinforcing, or supplementing material in the textbook.

Bulletin boards can solve the problem of how to teach students with different learning styles. Recent research in left brain and right brain dominance and learning styles, for example, indicates that scholastic underachievers (who may be quite bright) have difficulties at school since most instruction consists of teacher talk (lecturing, questioning, discussing). Because these students are usually tactile and kinesthetic, they learn best from a hands-on approach (13).* As Bruno observes, even in the general population,

> By far, the highest percent of students are tactile/kinesthetic and when these youngsters manipulate hands-on materials, they tend to remember more of the required information than through the use of any other sense. (6)

According to McCarthy (22), 82 percent of students fall into her Innovative, Dynamic, and Commonsense Quadrants. (An innovative learner needs personal involvement and social interaction; a dynamic learner needs a variety of activities and learns through

---

*Numbers in parentheses appearing in the text refer to the Bibliography beginning on page 79.

self-discovery; a commonsense learner learns through hands-on experiences.) Interactive bulletin boards can provide learning activities to meet all three learning styles. In addition, Stewart found that students in the general population chose games and projects as their preferred learning methods (29). Wasson reported that gifted students also preferred games as well as independent study (32). Level III bulletin boards (see Chapter 6) are like games and Level IV boards (see Chapter 7) are projects, either for groups or for independent learners.

Students can also relate to bulletin boards on different levels. Slower learners return to the board again and again for review—at their own pace. Less abstract thinkers appreciate the concrete materials and simply stated lesson themes. Active students respond to the hands-on activities, while creative learners relish the choices available. The same bulletin board can also include different levels of assignments.

Decorated walls can make students feel more welcome. They show the teacher's care of the environment and respect for order. They indicate prior planning, even if students themselves have made the bulletin board. They show that the teacher recognizes that some students learn differently from others and can benefit from additional teaching techniques. If the teacher is enthusiastic about a bulletin board, the students will catch that excitement and the resulting interest will add to the learning situation.

As students become involved in making bulletin boards, they can not only take over this classroom duty, but they can also be responsible for their own learning. Moreover, they teach each other naturally when they prepare bulletin boards for each other.

HELPING THE TEACHER

Most teachers would agree that a "beautiful bulletin board" is an asset to a classroom, but bulletin boards are low on their list of priorities. Teachers are busy with so many other tasks that making a bulletin board is the last thing they want to do.

Two considerations apply here:

1. If a bulletin board is to be an integral part of the lesson, it should be made first. Indeed, the bulletin board activity might be planned for the first day of a lesson (especially in

secondary classrooms when time is so limited). In this case, time preparing it would be well spent. And, if a relatively blank bulletin board is used (see p. 9), the setup is not complicated.
2. The teacher need not make the bulletin board. Others can help—a team of teachers on an in-service day, a paraprofessional, a volunteer, or, best of all, *the students themselves*. One teacher requires students to make a bulletin board as part of their regular classroom projects; throughout the year the boards are changed weekly (23).

The bulletin board can become the focal point of the lesson and can develop as you teach the unit. You can even start with all blank boards, using the lessons themselves to decorate your room; and as the days progress, using the ideas contained in this book. These ideas will make teaching easier since the bulletin boards will supplement and enhance your teaching, as well as keeping the topic clearly before the students. As students become more familiar with the way bulletin boards can work for them, they can take over more of the construction, thus relieving you of the work.

Using bulletin boards as teaching tools may mean a new organization for your classroom. Students will be moving about, looking through magazines and newspapers, cutting and pasting, spreading papers on the floor to plan, and talking together. This will mean a different kind of monitoring on your part: circulating to keep students on task, and becoming a research assistant as you "orchestrate" the learning activity. As students work cooperatively and make their own choices, the classroom atmosphere will become more informal and relaxed.

As interactive learning tools, bulletin boards are open-ended; that is, students choose what they will put up on them within the framework of the lesson. This gives students a freedom not found in traditional textbook worksheet assignments. In other words, students are allowed to express their creativity while learning responsibility (see Chapter 6).

As you begin to use bulletin boards as an integral part of your lesson plan, soon your walls will be filled, "spilling out" into the hallway. Colleagues will see your students bringing various materials from home to use on the bulletin boards. Your classroom will become very visible.

8

The principal will also notice these activities. A room with bulletin boards that follow the curriculum will immediately inform the principal about the topics being studied. Often a principal must show parents or school officials around the building, and a classroom with bulletin boards that reflect daily activities makes it easy for visitors to see what is happening in the room. Further, such bulletin boards indicate *active* student involvement in learning.

In the same way, parent-teacher conferences and Open House Night provide opportunities to share the classroom with parents. Teachers often display student work, but what better way to let parents know what is happening than bulletin boards that display the current topics under study? Especially if their child has been involved in using or making the board will parents appreciate the quick knowledge of the curriculum that a large visual affords them. They will see that the classroom walls are instructional as well as attractive.

As for construction—*you need not be an artist* to make successful bulletin boards. All that is needed is the desire to make them. Read a few books in the library about color and design to get a feel for layout and you'll be on your way. Better bulletin boards will come with practice. Start simply. Do not be overly concerned with aesthetics. Remember the main objective is to help students learn. Decide to try just one instructional bulletin board, and then relax and do it.

The cost is minimal: paper, pins, scissors, glue. If you do not have a bulletin board in your room, use butcher paper or plain shelf paper and attach it to the wall with duct tape. Or use large cardboard and either set it on tables or on the floor, depending upon your situation. Cubicles for bulletin board learning centers can be made from the cardboard from large boxes. Flannelgraphs are really bulletin boards; you can use felt instead of flannel, and sandpaper to attach items. As a teacher who traveled from room to room and even building to building, I made a bulletin board on a large sheet of paper, then rolled it up to carry to the next class.

The "perfect" bulletin board is blank. It may not be completely blank, but it will be *ready for use by students*. It may have colored paper and a title already affixed, but the actual construction will be done by students *during the lesson*, thus adding to the course of regular activities. Note the following example:

Food Groups

Make four large flashcards with the words "Meat," "Bread," "Milk," and "Fruits and Vegetables." Place them on the bulletin board in four areas, separated by lines or strips of paper. Have student find pictures of foods in magazines, cut them out, and pin them in the correct group. This activity can be used for secondary health, science, or home economics classes studying nutrition. For younger students, use the three meals, Breakfast, Lunch, and Dinner, as category headings.

This, then, is an "interactive bulletin board," one with which students interact, in a hands-on experience. Either teacher or students can plan it, but the work is done by students.

This book will help you plan bulletin boards that will help you teach. It will not tell you how to cut out letters, make "pretty" borders, or give essentials about layout and color. Information about these topics can be found in art books and commercially published bulletin board books. This publication shares the how to's of using bulletin boards in the classroom, making them illustrate lessons, serve as outlines for class discussions, become active learning tools for students, and enhance your teaching by involving your students in meaningful hands-on activities.

Chapter 2

USES OF BULLETIN BOARDS

Most classrooms are built with one or more bulletin boards, because school designers know that they are a part of education, if only for aesthetic value. What do bulletin boards do in a classroom?

ANNOUNCE

Inherent in their name, bulletin boards are used for bulletins. In most classrooms these usually include the school calendar, fire drill procedures, daily announcements, lunchroom menu, classroom rules. These general announcements do not relate to the subjects taught in the classroom. They should, of course, be kept current and be posted in a convenient but out-of-the-way location. Let students check these announcements themselves, thus conserving classroom time (23). Interactive bulletin boards, on the other hand, can announce a study topic to come, or capture the interest of students with a question or puzzle. These should relate directly to the curriculum and should be on the front board or in a place where they can be seen easily as students enter the classroom.

BEAUTIFY

Not only do bulletin boards display announcements, but if they are colorful and eye-catching, they will interest students in the curriculum as soon as they enter the classroom. Students like and need color. Look at your classroom with a decorator's eye as you would a room in your house; after all, you and your students "live" there most of the day. Read books on color; use colored paper for a background even for school announcements.

Some teachers fasten posters with various slogans to walls, attempting to make the classroom a more friendly place for students to enter. Other teachers put "READING IS FUN" in big letters across the top of the wall, hoping to motivate students to read. These types of bulletin boards do help to create a more attractive and comfortable atmosphere, but they do not relate to the topics under study.

DISPLAY

Sometimes student papers or pictures are posted in order to recognize and share achievement. One research study showed that students like to see their own work on the board, but do not notice the work of others (8). Certainly posting papers for the sole purpose of showing off fine handwriting or artistry will have limited appeal for those who are not so gifted. But papers that share in teaching the topic will be a valuable learning aid in advancing the subject matter, if used effectively. Students can also bring personal items from home that relate directly to subject matter to put on the bulletin board.

By displaying the teaching topic, the bulletin board serves as a constant reminder and reinforcement of the topic under discussion. Bulletin boards can also team up with an exhibit on a table in front of the board, adding words and pictures to the concrete objects on display. These display bulletin boards are Level I types (see Chapter 4). Note the following example:

Food Groups

The teacher makes this bulletin board, posting pictures of foods under the categories "Breads," "Meats," "Fruits and Vegetables," and "Milk." This serves as a visual example of the lecture.

DEMONSTRATE

A bulletin board can be used to demonstrate concepts visually, thus adding to the lecture and textbook readings. It can summarize a lesson, using the key words, perhaps adding arrows to show relationships.

Demonstration boards can be used during lessons more often than the display boards. They can be the jumping off points for discussions. You may add materials to them during your lecture, or students can use a worksheet with questions that the bulletin board will answer. These demonstration/discussion bulletin boards are Level II types (see Chapter 5). Note the following example:

Food Groups

On the Level II bulletin board, the teacher cuts out the pictures and adds them to the food group categories *while teaching* about each one. The bulletin board is an integral part of the lesson, but the teacher, not the students, is making it.

SHARE

Bulletin boards are ideal as cooperative learning projects. As students interact with bulletin boards, they work with others, whether looking in magazines for pictures to pin up, taking turns at the board, or planning, designing, and making the bulletin board as a group project. In learning centers, students can work alone or in pairs, depending upon the situation. As students help each other, peer tutoring occurs *naturally*, and both participants benefit. Open-ended bulletin boards plan automatically for social interaction.

INSTRUCT

Bulletin boards become vital learning tools as they move the lesson from the textbook to the wall. *Introduce* a topic to be studied by affixing large cutout letters announcing it and perhaps adding related pictures or maps. Or use a question, even one from the textbook, as an introductory discussion activity.

Motivate students by directing their attention to the bulletin board, using it as a jumping-off point for discussion or research. Place questions relating to the lesson on the board, hiding the answers, or use open-ended discussion questions. Post riddles or trick questions to attract attention. Note the following example:

For a lesson on fractions, write,

When does $1\frac{1}{3} + 3\frac{3}{4} = 4$?*

The bulletin board can *teach* the topic by outlining the points of the lesson; it can assist you by keeping your thoughts (as well as the students') organized. The bulletin board can serve as "notes"

---

*When reconstituting powdered milk.

for a lecture as you refer to it. You can add subtopics on flashcards as you speak, continuing the outline. Bulletin boards as learning centers give additional activities to reinforce a topic for students. When giving students a list of projects, include making a bulletin board as one of the choices.

Interactive bulletin boards *involve* students. With a plan and a setup, you can set students free to add the items they wish on a particular topic. They choose. They act. They make the bulletin board "theirs," thereby developing control of their own learning. They feel an ownership of the subject.

The bulletin board can also be *interdisciplinary*. As one subject blends into another, the board pulls them all together. Note the following example:

Food Groups

Multicultural. On the Food Groups bulletin board just described (p. 13), students add items from their homes that reflect their cultural heritage. This is particularly effective with mainstreamed English-as-a-Second-Language students, since they can make a unique contribution to the lesson.

Reading—Elementary. The day after putting up pictures of foods, students use newspapers and cut out words and pictures to add to the categories.

Reading—Secondary. Students find articles and recipes about certain food groups in newspapers and post them in the categories.

Math—Elementary. The following day, students find prices of the foods in the newspaper advertisements. They can pin these on the bulletin board also or do comparison shopping among the ads of different stores.

Math—Secondary. Students plan a balanced meal and figure the cost.

Although the bulletin board can do these things for students, the teacher must direct their attention to it and use it as an integral part of the lesson. It may take students some time to feel at ease using bulletin boards as learning tools since this may be a new way of learning for them. But don't be discouraged. Your enthusiasm is catching, and your students will learn how to interact with a bulletin board by your example.

Chapter 3

REVIEW OF THE LITERATURE

Bulletin boards have long been a standby in classrooms. Almost every room has one or more corkboards for teacher use. Magazine articles abound with ideas for "Successful Bulletin Boards." Most commercial publishing companies have at least one book on how to make bulletin boards, including sample border patterns, how to draw people, and letter-making guides. Universities and school districts have published booklets or guides to help teachers. Sample bulletin boards are specific to a topic or lesson. But what difference have bulletin boards made in the instruction of students?

RESEARCH STUDIES

Only two research studies about bulletin boards have been reported in the Educational Resource Information Center (ERIC [EJ 199 099]).

Collingford (8) extensively surveyed "top" juniors in Britain (nine- and ten-year-olds) to determine how much information was retained from bulletin board display of students' papers. Collingford was interested in two types of pupils' reactions to bulletin board displays: cognitive and emotional. In determining how much students learned from a display, he found that—

1. *Students do not learn automatically from information placed on the walls.*
   a. In 20 classes, only one student, after three weeks, was able to repeat a message (for a reward) that had been written in a child's hand and included in the display.
   b. Another paper was posted, containing new facts for the unit under study, but under a fictitious student's name. After three weeks, no one commented on it or knew any of the facts, except one girl.
   c. Still another paper, also with new facts, was prepared by the teacher and posted. After one week, no one could recall any of its facts when given a short test.

15

2. *Students think they remember what was on the walls when they do not.*

Seventy-five percent of the students queried said that they remembered the displays well and could recall them in detail. But not one student was able to give a single detail when asked to describe the boards. Yet these same students could describe their bedroom decoration in detail.

3. *Students remember the placement of their own work but no one else's.*

Students' poems were displayed and, after one week, were taken down. Then students were asked where various poems had been displayed. Ninety percent correctly placed their poems but could not recall either the content or placement of the poems of others.

Adults, including the principal or a supervisor, react emotionally to classroom decoration, as soon as they enter a room. Students may not remember details, but they too respond emotionally to bulletin board displays. Collingford found that—

1. *Although students have specific likes about certain places and pictures, they are vague about why they like them.* Over one hundred nine- and ten-year-olds were asked about their attitudes to visual impressions and places.
   a. Over 90 percent of the students said they had favorite places to be, some practical ("the television is there"), but most emotional ("nice decorations," "peace and quiet").
   b. Concerning pictures, they were not interested in content but in the general effect ("makes me feel good," or "cheerful").
   c. Students usually wanted a large number of pictures and posters because of the "general cheerful result."
   d. The majority agreed on one particular content: their own work, but only if mounted well.

2. *Students do not like bare clean walls.*

When questioned about classrooms that had no displays, but just clean white walls, students' reactions were very emotional. They had strong feelings of dislike, associating white walls with a prison-like atmosphere, using words like "cold," "miserable," "dull," and "bored."

In the second study, Creekmore (9) was concerned with the overstimulation that most primary classrooms give students, so much in fact, that they cannot absorb everything, which may increase off-task behavior. Looking at Piaget's theory that learning occurs when there is interaction between the learner and the environment, Creekmore developed a plan for efficient bulletin board use, using the front wall to introduce new material and the side walls for interactive and reinforcement activities.

Creekmore did a preliminary research study, using two teachers and two separate classrooms, and 20 mildly learning-impaired lower elementary students. Both teachers taught the same materials to their groups on 10 separate occasions, with identical lesson plans. They used the classroom with the bulletin board five times and the traditional room five times. Four times out of five, the students learning in the bulletin board room gained more than those in the traditional room; the fifth time, the gain was the same.

DISCUSSION OF RESEARCH

Collingford's study reveals that students want wall decorations, they want to see their own work displayed, but they do not learn merely from items being posted. Creekmore, however, found that interactive bulletin board work can make a difference in information retained.

Collingford's study vividly points out that merely putting students' work on the bulletin board makes no difference whatsoever in the learning process. In fact, he observes that it would be just as effective to use a visual during the lesson and then discard it, since once posted, items seem to be forgotten. This makes teacher use of bulletin boards especially important in the educational process— encouraging students to participate and use the boards as learning tools.

Collingford's studies may demonstrate the lack of value of posting students' papers, but Davies (11) disagrees. He believes that "Any display is better than no display," although he thinks the boards must be continually updated.

According to Collingford, students *do* want their own work posted, but they neither notice nor learn from other student papers. The fact that students could not describe details from classroom walls but could avidly discuss their own bedroom decorations indicates that when a display is meaningful to a student, perhaps even prepared by the student, the details are retained.

Creekmore, on the other hand, used interactive bulletin boards that involved the students. He noted some advances in acquisition, although, as he declared, it was only a preliminary study. He found that the traditional methods also showed gains, but the bulletin boards showed more. Creekmore overcame the usual research study problems of validity/reliability when studying teaching methods by using two teachers and two different but shared rooms. The additional problem of research with bulletin boards—the difficulty of preparation and portability—was solved by using the two rooms.

Why is so little research about classrooms use of bulletin boards available? Are teachers not using bulletin boards as active teaching/learning tools? Do bulletin boards take too much time to plan and prepare? Is it too difficult to prepare a bulletin board and *not* use it for part of the classroom in order to have a control group? How are students taught to select relevant information and display it effectively to others? What are teacher attitudes toward the use of bulletin boards?

Collingford invites teachers to repeat his experiments with students as well as with teachers and visitors for hallway displays. The difference in information retained when the teacher directs students' attention to the board needs to be explored. Creekmore's experiment also needs to be replicated and a statistical determination made of any significant differences.

What if a reward were offered in advance for finding a certain item? In my school hallway, a detailed bulletin board that included all the information in a chapter of the eighth grade history textbook about the Pilgrims and the New World contained a mistake. (The poster of the sailing ship representing the Mayflower had a small American flag.) The principal and the history teacher offered a reward to the first student to find the error. Each day, every hour, six or seven students stood at the board, searching for the mistake, and doublechecking every fact. It took two weeks for someone to find it. Throughout that time, student interest was high.

More research is needed on the relationship between students and bulletin boards. The studies of Collingford and Creekmore need to be replicated and improved upon. Other questions also need answers:

- Do bulletin boards increase student interest as well as achievement?
- Is it enough that students may *enjoy* learning with bulletin boards?
- What is the relationship between student learning style and retention of information from interactive bulletin boards?
- Do teacher attitudes toward bulletin boards determine student attitudes?
- Which types of bulletin boards do students remember over time and why?

In order to learn from bulletin boards, students need teacher guidance in their use; simply putting them up does not guarantee that students will even notice them. If students in the study were able to talk enthusiastically about their bedroom decorations, then the environment *is* important and can make a difference.

Students are naturally drawn to a bulletin board that offers a hands-on experience. My fourth graders fight over who gets to do the most work on a bulletin board; they do not recognize that the extensive map work we do is social studies, for example, since we are not reading the textbook and answering questions. Bulletin boards have served to *advance* their learning as they must use the maps to find more difficult items ("From the list of oceanic trenches in the almanac, find the deepest trenches in the sea floor by reading the latitude and longitude.") and practice skills (locating states). Could these topics have been taught as well and *as easily* with a text? I think not.

The following chapters provide detailed suggestions for planning and making bulletin boards for all subjects and grade levels to help both teaching and learning become more effective and enjoyable.

Chapter 4

LEVEL I: DISPLAY BULLETIN BOARDS

This chapter offers guidelines for making bulletin boards that instruct, that are more than just pretty pictures. Level I Bulletin Boards illustrate a topic. They may have diagrams, pictures, words, or materials from the current unit of study. You can use a Level I board to illustrate a lesson as you are teaching, directing students' attention to it during the lecture or learning activity. Students do not interact with the board directly; it is static and does not change during the lesson. Level I is the most commonly made instructional bulletin board; ironically, it takes the most teacher time to make. It is also the one most often described in magazines and commercially published bulletin board books.

GUIDELINES

To begin—

1. Decide to do it.

You want to increase students' learning, to grab their attention when they enter the room. You believe that an instructional bulletin board will do this. Make the decision to try to make one and then do it. This step is the most important for success. Overcome the obstacles of time, materials, and space. Make the bulletin board a first priority. Get someone to help if necessary.

2. Realize that students may not respond at first.

Students are used to ignoring the walls around them. They are used to the alphabet above the chalkboard, the "Rules of the Classroom" poster, the "Reading Is Fun" sign, the fire drill instructions. A bulletin board that is an integral part of the unit may be new to them. My first bulletin boards went unnoticed until they had been changed three times. At two weeks each, that meant I went six weeks before seeing a response from students. Expect this and then be pleasantly surprised the first time they notice one. Increase students' perception by actively directing their attention to the board as you teach, referring to it again and again.

3. Relax.

Don't worry about creating an artistic masterpiece. Concentrate on *content*, not pretty borders or fancy pictures. Realize that your bulletin boards will not only get better with experience but that they will *become easier*. If you feel doubtful or unsure of yourself, get together with another teacher to brainstorm together. Do not become discouraged. Remember your decision to do this and keep on.

4. Start simply.

Not only is it easier to put just a few items on the bulletin board, it is also more likely to attract the attention of students. Don't fuss with a border now, but do cover the bulletin board with a background of colored paper or cloth. Use the biggest letters possible and put up an introductory question, a vocabulary word, or a few words about a large poster that correlates with the study topic.

PROCEDURES

Selecting material for a bulletin board is the hardest part. It is an editing job and it may be difficult to choose just one idea. Personal likes and dislikes may be deciding factors, but that is all right. Choose something you like.

Step 1. Measure the bulletin board area.

The size of the bulletin board will determine what it will hold. Remember that items may extend out from the board, and may also be put on bare walls—any smooth surface will do (even the ceiling—see "Constellations," p. 68). If you do not have a bulletin board, use large pieces of cardboard or sheetrock, freestanding or on a table.

Step 2. Look at the subject matter under study.

Survey the objectives for the lesson. If you have not written them down, jot down the main points you plan to cover. Review the chapter in the textbook and any available supplementary materials for more ideas. Look at your audience—their learning levels, special needs, experiences, interests. Ask, "What am I trying to do with this bulletin board?" Develop at least one specific learning objective for each bulletin board.

Step 3. Look for an overall theme.

State the theme in one or two words. This can be displayed in foot-high letters above the chalkboard. Find an introductory question to lead students into the unit. Put it on sentence strips on a small front bulletin board. Do you have supplementary items that could be mounted with a brief description? Make large labels and arrange them neatly.

Review your lesson plan to see if any parts could be taught effectively on a bulletin board. Plan to use the board to present that material. The board will then be an integrated part of the lesson plan, not just an added feature.

Step 4. Gather materials.

Since the final form of the bulletin board will be determined by the materials available, examine all possible items—old pictures, souvenirs, and publications that might relate to the theme. Brainstorm with colleagues.

Be a scrounger. After you have exhausted the materials on hand, think of unconventional items: twigs, leaves, and bark; paper cups; cereal boxes; wood pieces, kitchen utensils; large envelopes; cloth of all kinds; doilies. Visit secondhand stores, garage sales, and variety stores with an open mind. Ask yourself, "How could I use this?"

Use *National Geographic* magazines. The foldout pictures in these publications are especially suitable for bulletin boards. Don't be squeamish about cutting pictures from the magazine. Most libraries have reference copies. It might be better to share your own issues with students on a display board rather than letting them sit unread on a shelf. Copies can also be found in used bookstores, secondhand stores, and at garage sales, sometimes for as little as ten cents each. Or ask for donations from the community. First look up your topic in the *National Geographic Index* at the library to know which issues to look for.

Keep supplies for making bulletin boards (scissors, markers, construction paper, glue, staples, pins) in a convenient place. Add other materials as you find them to your box or tote bag.

Step 5. Plan the bulletin board.

Lay out your collection of materials on a table. Which ones could work together to teach something about the unit? Select these items and place them on the floor in a measured area the size of the bulletin board. Think of a title that will correlate with the lesson and plan the size of the letters. Decide which labels you will add and the size they will be—larger for main points, smaller for details. Move the items around until they make a pleasing configuration. Decide on a background color. Draw a sketch of your layout to help in assembling the bulletin board.

If several items will not combine, concentrate on one item and build the board around it. Find related facts and write them on large colored squares or circles cut from construction paper. Use words that will increase students' vocabulary that you can refer to during class. Bulletin boards may relieve you of writing on the chalkboard, especially if you choose words that will be used frequently. As suggested above, move items around until you are satisfied with the arrangement; then draw a sketch.

If at first you have only words from the text, make them large in size and place colored geometric shapes behind them. This is a good way to begin, since it will attract students' attention and get your message across with no distractions. Later, when students expect to learn from the bulletin boards in your room, they will better appreciate more exotic materials and designs.

Lettering. Stencils seldom are large enough for titles. Preparing your own letters gives you more flexibility in sizes and styles. Letter patterns of varying sizes can be made of tagboard. Students can also help draw and cut out letters. If you cannot cut or draw letters freehand, then read a book on how to fold paper for cutting letters. Block letters are easiest, but corners can be rounded or curved, free-style letters can be cut and will not show flaws readily. Since I have trouble getting lines straight, I usually cut out letters rather than drawing them with markers directly on the board. This way if I make a mistake, I can move the letters around easily before pinning or stapling. I seldom place letters in a straight line but rotate each one slightly to avoid a distinguishing straight line that might be crooked, either because of my poor measuring, or a crooked wall or board. A string can be used as a guideline.

Step 6. Assemble the bulletin board.

Take all the materials and letters you have collected to the bulletin board. Put up the background (construction paper, colored paper from large rolls, newspaper, cloth, etc.). Since this is the most time-consuming part, I usually keep the same background for several boards. Using your diagram, begin pinning the items on the board, moving them around as needed, adding more words or colored shapes for greater attractiveness.

After attaching the materials, stand back and look carefully at the board. Try to see it as a student would. Ask yourself, Is it easy to read? Is it uncluttered? Do I get the main point? Does it look organized? Rearrange items if necessary, staple them on the board, and remove the pins.

Step 7. Use the Level I bulletin board.

During your lectures, remember that you have a bulletin board to help you. Refer to it often during each class period, calling attention to the vocabulary or pictures. Relate them to the unit so that students can make the connection. Change the words during the unit, if you wish, to keep the board up-to-date.

Step 8. Evaluate the bulletin board.

When the unit is over, look at the bulletin board again and ask, Did it serve its purpose? Was it helpful to me? Did I remember to use it? Did the students notice it and look at it when I directed their attention to it? Was it worth the time it took to make? What changes should be made for future use?

Since it does not change, a Level I bulletin board is usually outdated within two weeks. Try to change boards as often as that, either piecemeal or all at once. Or leave them blank for a few days—to alert students that a new one is coming (26).

Step 9. Save the bulletin board.

After evaluating the board, remove the material carefully and put it in a file folder or a large manila envelope with the sketch and the title marked on the outside. Laminate the material for durability, if possible. Store it in a place where it will not be crushed so that the letters and pictures will not need to be replaced.

EXAMPLES

The following pages contain examples of Level I bulletin boards for several subjects.

Math

Using Fractions

Find items from everyday life that use fractions and mount them on the board with labels—for example, tools, music, measuring cups and spoons, ruler, pie plate (marked off in sections), recipes, clock (20).

Social Studies

The Civil War

Affix pictures, postcards, maps, Confederate money, travel brochures, and a time line of events to the board. Use a blue background for the top half, gray for the bottom.

The English in the New World

Put up maps of Europe and America. Affix large cutout pictures of Pilgrims. Add a poster of an old sailing ship. Include pictures and travel brochures.

Science

Animal Phyla

Make category headings of the names of the animal phyla. Around them place pictures of representative examples. If desired, arrange the material in the form of a "Tree of Life."

How the Body Is Like a Machine

Draw an outline of the human body and a car, side by side. Label and draw arrows to associated parts, such as digestive system, gasoline lines; food, gasoline; brain, driver; skeleton, frame; sweat, exhaust.

Language Arts

Prepositions

Draw an outline or a stick figure of a person on the bulletin board. Add prepositions in the appropriate places: over, beside, on, in, behind, in front of.

Career Education

Which Job for You?

Put up pictures of people working at different jobs and label them. Add recruiting brochures or listings of job qualifications.

Chapter 5

LEVEL II: DISCUSSION BULLETIN BOARDS

This chapter provides information on how to prepare and use bulletin boards actively while you are teaching. Level II bulletin boards serve as springboards or guides to discussion. They may have specific or open-ended questions. During the presentation, you may be adding materials to these boards so that the lesson plan unfolds before the class. Students may also participate by using a worksheet with answers to be found on the board. In other words, Level II bulletin boards move the teaching and learning toward the wall more than the Level I boards.

Some of the same procedures used for Level I boards apply here. The teacher prepares the boards, and when complete, they will look like those at Level I. Level II boards require the same amount of time to plan and construct, but an added task is to keep certain materials—flashcards and worksheets—available and in order. Level II bulletin boards, however, are more useful during teaching time.

PROCEDURES

The steps for preparing a Level II bulletin board are similar to those for making a Level I board with some differences.

Step 1. Measure the bulletin board.

See Chapter 4. Level II bulletin boards must be within your reach, while Level I boards can be in many places—around the clock, above the doorway, or even on the ceiling. (See Chapter 4, Step 1.)

Step 2. Look at the subject matter under study.

See Chapter 4. Since you will be changing the Level II board as the lesson progresses, you may be able to plan to use more material than with the Level I board. Select the material that can best be taught on a bulletin board and include this activity as part of your lesson plan. Level II boards are integral parts of the lesson; material shared here may not need to be taught again. The bulletin board need *not* be supplementary (although it may be); but it is a valid teaching tool and can be used in lieu of other methods.

Step 3. Look for an overall theme.

See Chapter 4. When you identify the theme, look for more subtopics since Level II boards grow. You can specifically direct the discussion by adding new ideas to the board during the lesson.

Step 4. Gather materials.

See Chapter 4.

Step 5. Plan the bulletin board.

See Chapter 4. After deciding which materials to use, and how to arrange them, make a preliminary sketch. Then determine which materials to take *off* the board to be put on during the lesson. Leave on the decorative features: borders, shapes for color and background design, figures, and title. Especially at first, leave on enough to attract student attention. You may be adding pictures, captions, flashcards, three-dimensional materials. Take these off the board area and put them in separate piles. Draw another sketch. It should look like a skeleton of the finished bulletin board.

Step 6. Assemble the bulletin board.

See Chapter 4. Before the class begins, decide exactly when, in your lesson plan, you will use the bulletin board. Practice how you will put up the added materials. Make sure they fit and are arranged attractively. Take the materials down and leave the pins in the board. Put the materials in a convenient place where you can pick them up easily during class.

Step 7. Use the Level II bulletin board.

Level II bulletin boards are a useful substitute for writing on the chalkboard or overhead projector, and for showing examples, pic-

tures, and diagrams to students in a dynamic way. Taking the time to put items on the bulletin board also slows the pace of the lecture so that both teacher and students can take a breath. Be sure, however, that students are involved while you are putting the items on the board—writing the words, drawing the diagram, describing the picture. This affirms the bulletin board as a valid teaching tool (and also ensure students' attention). Put the materials up as practiced, talking about each one as you do so. Leave them up until the end of the lecture, referring to them often to reinforce the information. If a different class follows, take the materials down at the end of the period, so that they will be ready to use again. Note the following example:

Differences Between North and South

This bulletin board will be a chart. Add the title and headings, "North" and "South." Leave space on the left side for topics such as "Population," "Railroad Miles," "Size of Army," "Numbers of States," "Banking Capital," "'Property Values." Larger categories might be "Political," "Social," and "Economic." Make flashcards with the facts for each topic.

As you talk about each difference, add the flashcards. Students should take notes. The finished bulletin board will be a completed chart. It will look like a Level I board, except that it will contain too much information to put up at once. Therefore, the topic is best covered by a Level II board that grows with the discussion. The chart can serve as a reference for further discussion of the Civil War.

Step 8. Evaluate the bulletin board.

In addition to the questions given in Chapter 4 (p. 24), ask the following: Was it easy for me to use? How do I need to change my presentation of the board? Did students respond appropriately? Was the board useful during later discussions?

Step 9. Save the bulletin board.

See Chapter 4.

EXAMPLES

The following pages contain examples of Level II bulletin boards for several subjects.

Math

Candy Bar Math

To teach fractions, cut out a big sectional chocolate bar from brown paper. Cut the sections apart and label each 1/28. On sentence strips, write discussion questions: "What fractional part is two squares?" "How much does each square cost?" "Can you write questions about the candy?" Move the candy bar sections into the different groupings while teaching.

Roman Numerals

Make flashcards of Arabic numbers and the corresponding Roman numerals. As you teach, put up the matches, first for the single numerals, then for the more complicated combinations.

Social Studies

Time Line
(of any event)

On a large sheet of paper, mark off equal segments for as many years as desired. Make large flashcards and find pictures that match the historical events to be taught. Add them to the time line as you teach. (This is a way to demonstrate how to use a time line before students use one on their own.)

Science

What's Happening?

For a current events discussion, make large letters that say, "What's Happening in Science . . . Today . . . Yesterday . . . Tomorrow?" Include a time line and a world map. As you discuss scientific discoveries, show the locations where they occurred and relate them to past or future events.

Genetics and Inheritance

Set up the bulletin board with "P₁," "F₁," and "F₂" labels along one side (for generations). Make circles of paper, either color coded or labeled, for the traits being studied. Arrange these in the correct places, as you are teaching. After the lesson, take them down and use different material for the next lesson's examples.

Language Arts

Mythology—The Argo

Draw an outline map of the Mediterranean area on the bulletin board. Cut out a Greek sailing ship, the *Argo*, from paper and place it over the map. Write introductory questions on sentence strips: "Who sailed on the *Argo*?" "Where did it go?" As you read about its travels, mark the places on the map to show students.

Accounting

Balance Sheet

Make an enlarged balance sheet on the bulletin board, listing the accounts vertically on one side. Make flashcards with corresponding amounts of credits and debits, adding them to the board as you explain how a balance sheet works.

Chapter 6

LEVEL III: INTERACTIVE BULLETIN BOARDS

Interactive bulletin boards involve students completely. They were described earlier as hands-on activities in the classroom, reinforcing and supplementing regular textbook study. With these boards, students learn by doing.

Interactive bulletin boards mean a more relaxed classroom atmosphere; they have no time limits and, perhaps, no grades. Students have choices; they decide what the final bulletin board will look like. The teacher carefully plans the major lesson outlines and instructions, but the emphasis is to guide students to initiate their own instruction. Students develop self-confidence in drawing their own conclusions about how to do the assignment and how to achieve the lesson objectives.

Students may also interact with each other and the bulletin board, in pairs or small groups, in a noncompetitive environment. Interactive bulletin boards can be set up as learning centers to expand or review lesson objectives, and they may be worked on individually or cooperatively. If initial participation is voluntary, students will be more willing to try the activity (15).

PROCEDURES

Some Level I and II bulletin boards may be changed to become Level III. *Use* determines level. Teachers should not worry about *which* level they are using; they should use the bulletin board they need, the one that teaches their students most effectively. The steps used to construct Level III interactive bulletin boards are similar to those of Levels I and II, with some important differences.

Step 1. Measure the bulletin board.

See Chapter 4. This time, however, you must select a bulletin board that will be at the students' height, so that they can easily add or move materials around.

Step 2. Look at the subject matter under study.

See Chapters 4 and 5. Like Level II, a Level III bulletin board is an integral part of the lesson plan; indeed, it may be the *main* part of the lesson. Look at your objectives and determine where students might be able to make *choices* in the instruction. Can exercises be made open-ended? Is there an unlimited number of possibilities for filling categories? Are there charts, matching exercises, or diagrams with labels? Are there maps to locate places? Any of these instructional tools can become interactive bulletin boards.

Step 3. Look for an overall theme.

This is the key part of planning for an interactive bulletin board. Decide on your main objective and make a title for the board that reflects this theme. You may have details in mind, but students will be filling in details of their choice, so you must let go of the lesson plan here. You set it up and then free the students to do what they choose with it.

Step 4. Gather materials.

The final form of the bulletin board is determined by the materials students select to add to it. You may give them a narrow choice (a newspaper) or a wide choice (a large variety of items). Or you may ask them to search for their own materials. This step, then, determines how much control you will exercise over student choices. (The availability of appropriate materials may decide this for you.) Then, prepare items needed for student use and collect other necessary materials, such as newspapers and magazines.

Step 5. Plan the bulletin board.

You have your title and your materials. The question now is, how will students arrange the materials on the board? In a chart format? a collage? categories? Students need some guidance here and instructions must be simple.

Level III bulletin boards are the easiest for the teacher to make. In theory, you merely put up the title and cues to the activity (chart headings), choose the background color, and make the necessary cue cards.

However, more elaborate backgrounds or cues take more time. You may need to make flashcards for student use or compose a worksheet to go with the board. Be sure that these are ready for students if they are needed.

Step 6. Assemble the bulletin board.

See Chapter 4. Stand back and see if there is enough room for all students to become involved. Check the height of the board. Move materials as necessary. Put needed items within easy reach of students.

Thumbtacks or pins are usually used to attach items to bulletin boards. Thumbtacks are easier to use, but more unsightly; however, pins can be difficult to push into some boards. Buy pins with rounded tops; the extra expense will save fingertips. Also use a thimble. After materials are in place, static items can be stapled and the pins removed.

Pins can be a problem for student use, as they are potential weapons. At first, it may be necessary to guard the bulletin board to prevent the loss of pins.

For younger students, pockets to hold large cards are easy to use. Cards with large holes can be hung on hooks, pushpins, or nails, and moved around easily.

Other ways to affix materials include the use of masking tape, Velcro, stick wax, flannel, felt, sandpaper, strings, clothespins, magnets, and staples (25).

Step 7. Use the Level III bulletin board.

Check your lesson plan to make sure that you lead up to the bulletin board activity logically and that students have the necessary background to complete it successfully. Give instructions and demonstrate how to use the board. Then stand back. If this is their first experience with an interactive board, students may be shy.

Let students work at their own speed. Be available for help, but always let students make the decisions. Circulate to keep students on task. Be encouraging; as this is a hands-on learning/thinking activity, they need to be assured that they are doing well. Marvel when a student is ingenious—this will happen. Encourage creativity. Note the following example:

Introductory Board. Place the title "Our City" on the bulletin board and add travel brochures and postcards of the city.

Interactive Board. Remove the pictures, leaving the board blank, except for the title. Distribute newspapers. Ask students to find and cut out pictures or words about their city and pin them anywhere on the board.

Grading. Whether or not you give a grade for the interactive bulletin board will depend upon the activity. If there is a "right" answer, as in a matching or labeling game, then a score can be recorded. Rather than just marking the answers right and wrong, however, you might say something like, "Oops! Not all of them are correct!" and then let students doublecheck items and move the materials again. This gives students responsibility for learning and ensures that the activity will not be done hurriedly. This working through of an activity is where real learning occurs and students achieve success on their own.

Sometimes students are on their honor to try to do their best (for example, when checking their own work). If material is consistently found in the wrong places, have students divide into small groups for better monitoring, or after a time, test for the information. (Individuals can also take the test on the bulletin board.)

Many bulletin boards are self-checking. The answers are hidden (i.e., under the flashcard) so that students can have immediate feedback. For these boards, you merely check that the activity was completed.

During open-ended activities, which give students more choices, again, a mark that the activity was completed is enough. Cooperative learning activities mean that students will be helping each other without thought of grading; thus, real learning occurs as students achieve success working through the activity with friends. Thus a grade would be inappropriate.

Followup. A Level III bulletin board usually needs a followup activity or discussion to bring students' different experiences together. This can include giving the answers (as in a matching or categorizing activity), discussing why students chose the items, or summarizing student findings. Note the following example:

35

After students complete the newspaper search, have them discuss why they chose what they did. Categorize the words and pictures of buildings, stores, sports.

Step 8. Evaluate the bulletin board.

See Chapters 4 and 5. Ask, Were the students involved? Did they achieve the learning objective? Was I able to relate the activity to the rest of the unit lessons?

Step 9. Save the bulletin board.

This time you may not want to save all the pictures/newspaper articles students found. Or you may wish to add the items to your picture file. Sometimes, students may want to take home their contributions. If you used premade materials, such as flashcards, save these as for Levels I and II bulletin boards.

EXAMPLES

The following pages contain examples of Level III bulletin boards for several subjects.

Math

Geometry Around the World

Finds posters of cities. Place clear plastic pages over the posters. locate geometric shapes (in buildings), and outline them with a permanent marker. Remove the plastic and cut apart the geometric figures. Put these in envelopes under the corresponding posters. Have students choose a shape and move it around the poster to find a match.

Place Value

Put the word "Number" on the bulletin board, leaving a space after it for a large flashcard with a one-, two-, three-, or four-digit number of your choice (e.g., 4, 12, 307, 5,483). Below that, add the words "Thousands," "Hundreds," "Tens," "Ones," leaving space above each word for a flashcard. Fill an envelope with flashcards containing single-digit numbers. Have students choose a number from the envelope, read it aloud, and place the flashcard above the correct place value. Continue until the original number is completed. Change the number and repeat. This activity may be expanded to include larger numbers—ten thousands, hundred thousands, and millions.

Social Studies

Let's Go Around the World

Put a map of the world on the bulletin board. Around it, place the following: flags of countries, cards with countries' names; newspaper articles about the countries. On the map, students are to find these countries. They can use yarn to locate the country, move the cards, or just indicate the location. This board can move from one topic (flags, articles) to another, continually reinforcing country names and locations.

Chart of Countries

List country names vertically on one side of the bulletin board and attributes horizontally across the top (i.e., weather, geography, economy, population). Each student studies a country, researching its characteristics, finding or drawing pictures, or writing about these attributes. Then students put their information on the chart, under the correct heading.

If equal-sized papers are used for each attribute, they can be removed or changed and students can return them to the appropriate spot for testing or reinforcement (18).

Science

Body Parts

Each student lies on the floor and has a friend trace his/her body shape on a large paper. Post all these "bodies" around the room. As they study internal organs and systems, students draw, label, and cut out the parts and glue them onto their body.

Types of Clouds

On a blue background, label one side of the bulletin board with the altitude from 1,000 to 10,000 meters. Ask students to research and choose the type of cloud to draw, cut out, and affix to the board at the proper altitude. They may also use pictures of clouds from magazines.

37

Language Arts

Parts of Speech

Add to the bulletin board a sentence written on a sentence strip. In an envelope below place cards with the names of parts of speech—noun, verb, preposition, adjective, etc. Ask students to draw a card and place it above the word that matches the part of speech.

Greek and Roman Mythology: Gods and Goddesses

Make flashcards with the names of the Greek and Roman gods and goddesses. On one side of the bulletin board, list the types of gods (War, Love, Thunder, Sea). Students match names to types.

Home Economics

House

Make an outline of a house. Have students cut out pictures of furniture from magazines and place them in the rooms of the house. Then, ask them to make flashcard labels for vocabulary/spelling, or go to newspaper advertisements or department store catalogs and find the prices, and calculate the cost of furnishing a room/house.

Reading

Can You Make a Word?

Put pairs of hooks or sturdy pins on the bulletin board. Then make flashcards with words like "can," "pan," "brow," "eat," and with letters such as "e," "n," "b," "en," depending upon what is being studied. Have students add the letters to the words to make new words.

Foreign Language

Graffiti

Put a large blank paper on the bulletin board. Allow a short time each day for students to write jokes, sayings, proverbs, notes, and replies on the bulletin board, but only in the foreign language being studied. This is a good introductory activity (27).

Physical Education

Math in Sports

Put a picture of a sports figure on the bulletin board. Include a clipping from the newspaper, listing batting average (for a baseball player), football statistics (for a football player). Post questions such as, "His batting average is .375. Who is he?" "He has completed 15 passes, covering 1780 yards. Who is he?" Students must find the answers. Then let them make up questions for each other (7).

Hand-Motor Skills

Button! Button!

Put items on the bulletin board that teach early hand-eye-motor coordination skills—for example, a button and button hole, Velcro closing, shoelace to tie, snaps, a zipper. Have students take turns going to the board and practicing these skills.

Chapter 7

LEVEL IV: STUDENT-MADE BULLETIN BOARDS

The ultimate learning experience is creating a product that conveys meaning to the student who makes it as well as to classmates. Student-made bulletin boards are instructional tools for the whole class; thus, they serve a real audience—they are not made just for a grade from a "teacher audience." Students who plan and construct instructional bulletin boards have reason to be proud of themselves: they have taken the responsibility for their own learning and shared it with others.

Students can make bulletin boards of any level for classroom use: Level I—Display (Chapter 4), Level II—Discussion (Chapter 5), or Level III—Interactive (Chapter 6). All levels provide the opportunity to make choices and set priorities about the kind of information to include, and to create an effective medium for that information. Level I gives students the most control over what will be displayed, but, also, the most design work. Level II allows students a chance to supplement a discussion or lesson. It can assist them in making an oral presentation. In making a Level III board, students open up the subject matter to new interpretations by classmates as they participate in the activity.

GUIDELINES

How do teachers guide students to make instructional bulletin boards?

1. Be an example.

If you have made and used a variety of bulletin boards throughout the year, students will be more interested in making one themselves. Teacher enthusiasm is contagious. Students will see that they can learn through a bulletin board activity, perhaps just as effectively as from a textbook assignment. They will begin to understand the importance of visuals in education.

2. Critique.

Help students interpret what makes an effective display. Gather resource books about color and layout for them to read and then let them analyze the classroom bulletin boards. (Be prepared to take constructive criticism graciously.) If you do this for several boards, students will form their own opinions of effective displays.

3. Demonstrate.

Show students how you go about making a bulletin board. Share the steps listed in Chapters 4, 5, and 6. Tell them where they can get materials.

4. Brainstorm.

Brainstorm ideas with students. When you are studying a topic, lead them to think of as many different ways to present it as possible. Ask what materials they would like to use and help them find unique items. Encourage them to take risks and try something different. Be a guide and helper as they struggle with their own ideas.

5. Be specific.

Although you want to give your students as much freedom as possible, they will need specific guidelines to get started. The steps outlined in Chapters 4, 5, and 6 will help, but students will also need due dates for putting up and taking down bulletin boards. Particularly at first, they will need milestone dates for specifics: Objectives, Materials List, Materials Gathered, Sketch of Plan, Class Procedure.

With experience, students can carry out these steps on their own, but you will need to monitor groups and individuals to keep them on task.

6. Allow time.

Allow students time and space to work. Thinking, planning, prioritizing information, assembling, and arranging take time. Students will want to share their experience with their peers—by talking. Schedule "open time" in the lesson plan to provide students the opportunity to choose between various learning activities, including making a bulletin board.

7. Require a rough draft.

Require students to have the bulletin board ready before the display date so that they can lay it out (on the floor) and critique it. Give them a checklist developed from the evaluation questions on pp. 24, 29, and 36. Classmates can make suggestions for changes. Poor layout and illegible lettering will show up at this point, allowing time for correction before the display date.

8. Display the final bulletin board.

After students have made corrections on their rough draft, they mount their bulletin board. You may want to grade the project (and perhaps use a checklist similar to other evaluation lists).

If students have done their best, met all the deadlines, and reached the board's objectives, then certainly, no matter the artistic quality, the bulletin board will deserve a high grade. Aesthetics does play a role in effectiveness, however. Failure to make the rough draft will obviously affect the final form and, therefore, the grade.

Remember that bulletin board artists are not just cutting and pasting; they must distinguish main ideas from subordinate ones, and figure out how to clarify and express those ideas well. These are difficult tasks. Bulletin boards give students time to *think*, to contemplate new ideas—unlike the rush of overheads, slides, and workbook pages they often encounter (28). An organized plan that first demonstrates and then carefully guides students through the process will ensure success when they try making their own boards independently.

Chapter 8

A PRACTICAL APPLICATION: BULLETIN BOARD MAPS ACROSS THE CURRICULUM

To illustrate the use of bulletin boards in content areas, this chapter takes one concept—mapping—and uses it in examples of interactive bulletin boards for each subject area and for each grade level. I have chosen mapping, because not only is knowledge of geography vital to understanding the world, but recent tests have shown a surprising lack of such knowledge across age levels, reaching even into the college and adult years (10, 21). In addition, the mental visualization of places and concepts is a thinking skill useful for sorting out situations in a complex society and world.

Maps are symbols or ideas of reality. They need not be just representations of the earth; they may be tracings of concepts. This chapter defines mapping in its broadest sense: the study of anything across space—words or facts as they relate to one another; a story sequence; interactions between people, offices, or things; flowcharts; tree- or pyramid-shaped conceptions of ideas; time lines. As all the content areas are represented by map examples, many will interrelate, automatically creating interdisciplinary activities.

Most of these bulletin boards will be almost blank before students start working with them. Teachers who make the boards usually just set them up for student use by drawing a simple diagram on the background paper and perhaps adding a title (or letting students decide upon the title after the board is finished). Most of these examples may also be prepared by students on either the classroom bulletin board or on smaller poster boards.

Three figures provide overviews of suggestions for mapping activities—Figure 1 for kindergarten through grade three, Figure 2 for grades four through eight, and Figure 3 for grades nine through twelve. These are suggestions only. Although they specify grade level and subject, they can be adjusted for use at higher or lower grade levels. Some of the boards listed may seem to be too advanced for the designated age group. However, as soon as a top-

Grade Level	Reading/Language Arts	Social Studies	Mathematics	Science	Other Activities
K–3	Dot to Dot		Community Maps		Child Development Time Line
	Sequencing a Story	Garden Map	Floor Map	Dinosaur Habitats	Orchestra/Band Seating
	Student Vacation Trips	Cities/Countries of the World	Math Mail	Life Cycle of Animals	Table Setting
	Three-Ring Circus	Continents	Multiplication Tables	Solar System	
		Food Map		Space Exploration	
		Houses Around the World		Weather Maps	
		Pirate Maps			
		Room Map			
		School Map			
		Treasure Maps			
		Your House—Where?			

Figure 1. Bulletin Board Maps for K–3

44

Grade Level	Reading/Language Arts	Social Studies	Mathematics	Science	Other Activities
4–8	Mythology Travels	American Mosaic	Areas and Perimeters	Atoms	The Book Company
	Newspaper Publishing Flowchart	Christmas Around the World	Enlarging Patterns	Biomes of Life	Clothing and Design
	Regional Folk Heroes/Heroines	Continents	Exchange Rates	Body Maps	Design and Layout
	Semantic Maps	Election Trail	Geometry Geoboard	Constellations	Drug Map
	Story Grammars/Maps	Government Leaders	Graphing Quadrants	Contour Mapping	Music in Time and Space
		How a Bill Becomes a Law	History of Numbers	Earthquakes	Sports from Other Countries
		Immigration Routes	Interest Rates	Glaciers	Typewriter Keys
		Interstate Highways	Metric Conversions	Light Bulbs	Where Are Those Songs?
		Longitude and Latitude	Scales of Miles	Microscope	
		The Main Idea in Current Events	Sundials	Rain Forests	
		Newspaper Maps	Time Zones	Ring of Fire	
		Our State	Weather Maps	State Geology	
		Railroads Today and Yesterday	Where Does Your Money Go?	The U.S.A. at Night	
		Triangular Trade		Volcanoes	
				Water Cycle	

Figure 2. Bulletin Board Maps for Grades 4–8

45

Grade Level	Reading/Language Arts	Social Studies	Mathematics	Science	Other Activities
9–12	Arthurian Britain Novel Locations Origins of Fairy Tales Origins of Language Space Travel in Literature Storyboards Where Authors Live	Air Traffic Control Lanes Battlefield City Subway Community Maps Corporate Structures Food Distribution The History of Transportation The Mission Trail Mystery Maps Rivers World History Today	Air Traffic Lanes Geometric Shapes Hyperspace Calculations International Trade Latitude and Longitude Roads and Circles Rocketry Scatter Diagram Taking a "Pole" of the Class Your Initials in Parabolas	Animal Migration Atomic Energy: Production and Disposal Bending Light Chromosome Mapping Circuits of Technology DNA-RNA Flannelgraph Electric Fields Electricity Hit It! Land Navigation Parts of a Beach Periodic Table Photography Flowchart Rocks—Where Are They? Roller Coasters Tectonic Plates Tidepool Life Tides Where Are the Elements? Will It Move?	Blocking Careers Circles of Influence Community Businesses Football The Homeless Marching Band Formations Newspaper Galleys Shopping Malls Store Layouts What If . . ?

Figure 3. Bulletin Board Maps for Grades 9–12

ic is introduced, a hands-on bulletin board can be made to help students visualize the subject. Most of the boards are multilevel—they can apply to several grades or to several learning levels in one room. They are suitable for whole-class, small-group, or individual work. These examples can also serve as stimuli for ideas for other boards to fit individual needs.

The following pages contain brief descriptions of these examples. First, there are three sample activities for K-3 students—Dot to Dot (a premapping activity), and Community Map, and The Garden Map (two interdisciplinary activities). Then, there are descriptions of the remaining activities listed in Figures 1, 2, and 3. These are arranged by subject and subdivided into grade levels.

PREMAPPING

Dot to Dot

As a premapping exercise for kindergartners, select an animal form from an activity book. Put pushpins on the bulletin board in the shape of the design and add cards with either numbers or letters, depending on the subject being studied. Attach a long piece of yarn to number "one" or letter "A." Have students wrap the yarn around the pushpins in the correct order to make the shape.

INTERDISCIPLINARY MAPS

Community Map

This is an interdisciplinary activity for grades K-3. The map can be left up during the year and changed as students learn new skills. Students needing reinforcement of previously taught skills can continue to use it as a learning center, with materials from earlier lessons, at the same time that others are using it for different activities.

With a ruler, draw wide streets and intersections on the bulletin board. Have students make paper houses, stores, and street signs from construction paper and put them along the streets. Include a large traffic light. Start with just a few items, add and change items as the year progresses.

Safety. Have students make small paper figures of themselves. Moving them around the map, students can role play in small groups crossing the street, learning traffic light signals, walking from place to place, talking to community helpers (and *not* talking to strangers!). They can also make these additional paper figures.

Reading. Make flashcards with the names of all the pieces on the map. Have students match the labels with the items. The vocabulary can change with different study topics—for example, crosswalk, house, grocery store, school, stop, children playing, police officer, firefighter, street names.

For older students, play a "Directions" game to learn to give directions. Each student tells the directions to a spot on the map to a partner, who then must trace the way with a finger.

Write language experience stories about how to cross the street or make up a story about traffic lights or other community events.

Math. Have students go to the board in pairs and ask each other to count items: the number of buildings, the number of people, the number of streets. Add street numbers for reading larger numbers.

Have older students make more streets and number them, so that each pupil has a set of street signs to put on the board.

Have advanced students find newspaper ads of local businesses and place them on the community map in the correct places.

Story Problems. Story problems integrate reading with math skills. Using their own names, ask students to make up problems: "Jenny lives _____ blocks from school." "Does Marci live closer to the school or to the zoo?"

Science. Let part of the map be a zoo, where children can affix cutout paper animals or pictures from magazines. Include correct habitats, if possible, and labels for vocabulary.

Follow up this activity with a walk around the community, noting safety procedures, reading street signs, talking with community helpers, counting objects along the way. Visit the zoo. Return and put more items on the bulletin board map.

Have advanced students take compasses and find directions (2).

The Garden Map

Like the Community Map, this is an interdisciplinary activity for grades K-3. This map can also be left on the board all year and changed as students learn new skills. Those needing reinforcement of previously taught skills can continue to use it as a learning center, with materials from earlier lessons. A *correlated activity* could be growing seeds.

Using a brown paper background, mark off a large square to indicate the garden area. For younger students, you might need to mark off the rows. This is an example of a "blank" bulletin board, ready to go to work, with or without a title.

Discuss gardens and let students decide what kind of seeds they want to "plant." They can then draw and cut out their plants and pin them on the bulletin board. Use as many items as space permits. Place like items in the same rows.

The plant drawings may be of different sizes. The important thing is that students do the activity themselves and feel a part of it. The learning of content skills through talking and working together is stressed here—not artistic merit. Lead the way by accepting whatever students make and find something good about each contribution.

Reading. Make labels for the plants. Have students match the labels with the garden rows. The vocabulary will change as different items are planted. Have seed packages available for advanced readers. Then students can write about how to plant a garden.

Math. Ask younger students to count the number of each type of plant; have older ones multiply the number of plants by rows, and figure the ratio of each type of plant to the total number of plants. Each plant needs a certain space to grow; advanced students can figure the area needed, and thin the rows.

Story Problems. Using math, reading, and writing skills, students can make up word problems about the garden and let a friend answer them. These will be automatically individualized and can be as easy or as difficult as students make them. For example, "If you plant three seeds in two rows, how many seeds will you plant?" or "If 60 percent of the flower seeds planted will bloom, and you planted 476 seeds, how many seeds will bloom?" (30).

Science. Using reference books or seed packages, students can research and add cards that tell the depth each seed needs for planting, the best months for planting, and how long it takes to grow.

As a followup, plant a garden. If this cannot be done at school, encourage students to plant one at home with their parents.

49

READING/LANGUAGE ARTS

K–3

Sequencing a Story

To model the activity, during a language experience, ask students to share events in a story. At first, just list the events on the chalkboard as students remember them. Then let students copy the sentences on large squares of paper. Place the squares on the bulletin board in chronological order, changing them as students remember other happenings or doublecheck the story in their books. Later, students can do this activity themselves to share stories with each other. Younger students can draw pictures of the events and sequence them on the bulletin board.

Student Vacation Trips

Place a large map of the United States on the bulletin board. When students are out of school for a family vacation, ask them to keep a journal of their travels and collect postcards and travel brochures of the places they go. Then, when they return, have them plot their trip on the map with pins, yarn, or labels; attach postcards and souvenirs; and tell and/or write about it.

Three-Ring Circus

During a circus unit, draw three large circles on the bulletin board. Students can draw figures and animals to fit into the "rings," and make flashcards for learning the vocabulary. They can also role play a circus using the figures.

Grades 4–8

Some of these bulletin board suggestions may also be appropriate for advanced students in grades 1-3, or for slower learners in the upper grades. In addition, students can prepare written reports about most of the bulletin boards in other disciplines.

Mythology Travels

While reading myths, students can plot the travels of the characters on a map, comparing journeys. As students write their own myths, they can also plot their characters' travels.

Newspaper Publishing Flowchart

After visiting the local newspaper office, students can chart the process of publishing from the news happening through the delivery of the paper to the reader.

Regional Folk Heroes/Heroines

While reading folktales, students can draw pictures of the heroes/heroines and place them on a bulletin board map showing where they lived.

Semantic Maps

Cover the bulletin board with paper. In the middle of the board, write a word. Ask students to think of related words and write them on flashcards. Discuss categories for the words and put them on the board in groups, connected by lines to the main word. Brainstorm more words. Leave the semantic map on the board and let students add more words throughout the lesson. Add other categories and change them as the map grows.

Students may use the board to make their own semantic maps using lists of vocabulary words written on flashcards. They can move them around, adding more words, connectors, and categories (24).

Story Grammars/Maps

Story grammars or story maps are visualizations of story outlines, sequencing events, showing relationships, and causes and effects. First, the teacher demonstrates mapping for a story read in class with a Level II bulletin board. Then students make their own story maps. More than one story can be mapped on the bulletin board at the same time. Students can also use the board to brainstorm new story ideas to share and add to others. Possible categories are Setting, Time, Characters, Plot, First event, Conflict, Resolution, Ending. (See Guthrie [17].)

Some of these bulletin board suggestions may also be appropriate for advanced students in grades 6-8. Slower high school learners can also use boards suggested for the lower grades. In addition, students can prepare written reports about most of the bulletin boards in other disciplines.

Arthurian Britain

Students can research the historical King Arthur while reading the literature. The mapping task can include historical references, both traditional and archaeological, differences in names and places, as well as differing placements of Camelot, Camlan, Badon, for example. As students plot places, they can list details of the locations on 3 x 5 cards.

Novel Locations

Not only can students use published poster maps of fantasy literature (i.e., *The Land of Oz*, *Middle-Earth*, *Narnia*), they can also make their own maps of the literature they read that does not have maps available.

Add maps of poetry topics (for example, "Xanadu," "Dream-Land," "El Dorado" (12).

Origins of Fairy Tales

As students read fairy tales (or folktales), they can mark a world map showing where each one originated. In the case of a fairy tale common to many countries (such as *Cinderella*), have them research the many countries in which it is found, as well as the variations it has taken, and mark these on the map (19).

Origins of Language

Students can research world languages and place examples of these on the bulletin board map. They can show the migration of languages with arrows. They can also develop a "language tree" to show the relationships between languages.

Space Travel in Literature

Science fiction uses various names for hyperspace, warpspeed, or lightspeed, etc. Finding the references in literature, students can draw and label maps, adding planets, orbits, and distances as desired (see especially Asimov's *Foundation's Edge* [Doubleday, 1982]). Then they can use math skills to plot trips through space (see "Hyperspace Calculations," p. 64).

Storyboards

As students prepare to write their own stories, they can illustrate events sequentially and post them on the bulletin board, similar to the storyboards used in planning motion pictures. Then they can tell the story to the rest of the class, using the pictures as cues.

Where Authors Live/Lived

As students read novels and short stories, they can find where and when the authors lived and add this information to the bulletin board. Note: Pulitzer Prize winners, dates, and genre can also be plotted.

SOCIAL STUDIES

K-3

Cities/Countries of the World

Prepare a bulletin board for each country or city studied. Gather maps, posters, pictures, and fact cards and make up questions that can be answered from the information on the bulletin board. Questions can be in the form of a worksheet, on cards in an envelope attached to the board, or on large cards on the board near the maps/pictures and the answers. Students search the bulletin board for the answers and write them down.

Continents

For this introductory map activity, place a world map on the bulletin board. Hand out flashcards labeled with the names of continents. Ask students to locate the continents and pin the flashcards to the correct locations.

Food Map

Place a world map on the bulletin board. Have students draw small pictures of foods they (or their parents) eat that come from other countries (or other areas of the United States) and affix them to the correct place on the map.

Houses Around the World

Place a large world map on the bulletin board. Have students draw pictures of houses from other cultures, cut them out, and mount them on tagboard. Then have them trade with another student and try to find the correct countries.

Pirate Maps

Draw the coastlines of North and Central America, Europe, and Africa. As students study different pirate personalities, they can mark the routes and campaigns, and note shipwreck locations (16). Also include modern-day shipwrecks and their excavations such as the *Titanic* (3).

Room Map

For a kindergarten or first grade activity, mark off a large square on the bulletin board and draw in the classroom furniture, including student desks. Have each student bring a picture from home and add it with his or her name to the appropriate desk.

For an opening day activity, let more advanced students measure the furniture and cut out scale models to pin on the map. Assign each student a desk, plus another classroom article—a flag, a window, a bookcase. Students also can add their names to these. The furniture can be rearranged during a discussion of space efficiency. (The level of difficulty in drawing the items to scale will depend upon the students' levels.)

School Map

This activity is similar to the Room Map, except that students measure the rooms in the school and make a map to scale. Younger student can label an enlarged blank school map. Assign different rooms to different students. As a vocabulary exercise, use flashcards that can be taken off the board and replaced.

Treasure Maps

On a blank bulletin board, have students take turns placing their own cutouts of a compass direction, islands, trees, paths, bushes, rivers, ships, buildings, and X's for steps. Students decide where their "treasure" is buried. They write instructions for other students ("Take five steps east from the tree.") and draw a small replica map for an answer key. Then they take turns finding each other's "treasures."

Your House, Where?

Place a city or neighborhood street map on the bulletin board. Let students pin flags to the board to show where their houses are. Then, have them trace their route to school, with a finger, telling a friend, and then writing it down.

Grades 4-8

Some of these bulletin board suggestions may also be appropriate for advanced students in grades 1-3, or for slower learners in the upper grades.

American Mosaic

Post separate maps of each continent on the bulletin board.

Day 1: Ask students to make a family tree of their ancestors and find out where they were from.

Day 2: After they make small paper flags and put them on pins, have students write their ancestors' names on the flags. Then they can find the countries they were from on the bulletin board maps and pin the flags to those countries.

Day 3: *Math Followup*. Graph the last two generations on the bulletin board by country. Give each child enough squares on which to write parents' and grandparents' names.

Christmas Around the World

Students read and illustrate how different cultures celebrate Christmas. Then they post their pictures on the world map on the bulletin board and report on them.

Continents

Post a large world map on the bulletin board. Ask students to look in the newspaper for articles from all the continents, cut them out, and place them near the continent (20). This activity can also be done for all states in the United States.

Election Trail

During a presidential election year, post a large U.S. map on the bulletin board. Using four different colors of paper (one for each presidential and vice presidential candidate), let students make small flags to place on pins. Each time a candidate visits a town, post the appropriate flag on the map with the date. *Note*: This can also be done during state primary elections.

Government Leaders

Place a world map on the bulletin board. Using either pictures from magazines or names on flashcards, ask students to match government leaders around the world with their countries.

How a Bill Becomes a Law

Have students make large placards denoting the steps required for a bill to become a federal law (i.e., committee, House, Senate, presidential signature or veto, etc.). Then they place these on the bulletin board, in order, and add the names of the people involved. For example, if the bill deals with education, they can list the name of the Secretary of Education, the names of the committee members and their local congressional representative and how he/she voted.

Immigration Routes

Students can show the immigration of groups of people over time with arrows, dated and labeled, added to a world map. The map can illustrate migrations from the earliest times up to recent waves. Students can also add the reasons why people moved.

Interstate Highways

Post a blank U.S. map on the bulletin board. Ask students to draw in the interstate highways and put the numbers on little cards (cut in the shape of the interstate symbol). *Note*: First, draw the outline of your state and let students find the interstates. They may also add the U.S. routes. Show students a highway map to distinguish between U.S. and state route numbers.

Longitude and Latitude

Place a world map that shows longitude and latitude on the bulletin board. Make cards that list the degrees of longitude and latitude for cities around the world. Put the cards in an envelope and attach it near the map. Ask students to read the cards and find the cities on the map.

The Main Idea in Current Events

Post a U.S. map on the bulletin board. Give each student a recent newspaper. Ask students to read articles, find the main idea, and write it in one or two words on small paper flags. On the back of the flag, they should write the name of the city and find it on the bulletin board. This lesson will automatically indicate the locations of major news happenings.

Newspaper Maps

Place a large world map on the bulletin board. As students find maps of countries in newspapers, they should cut them out and place them on the world map in the correct location. Compare the different map legends and scales.

Our State

Post a large state map on the bulletin board. Cover it with clear adhesive plastic.

1. Ask students to cut out the names of cities in the state from the newspaper and put them on the map in the correct place with transparent tape. *Note*: This can also be done with a U.S. or world map.

See also activities for "Our City," pages 35–36.

2. As you study the state, have students draw or find pictures of products, animals, geography, poems, words, and political leaders

57

of the state and add them to the map.

3. Make packets of questions and activities available at all times so that the bulletin board is used as a multipurpose learning center as well as a whole-class activity. Write questions on different levels for multilevel classes.

Railroads Today and Yesterday

On a U.S. map, ask students to put up small "tracks" cut out of paper to show major railroad routes. As they study U.S. history, they can post the early railroad lines and point out their economic, social, and political impact.

Triangular Trade

Post a map of the Atlantic Ocean and its coastlines on the bulletin board. Let students make small paper ships and move them along the routes of the early colonial traders between England, Africa, the West Indies, and the colonies.

Grades 9–12

Some of these bulletin board suggestions may be appropriate for advanced students in grades 6–8. Slower high school learners can also use boards suggested for the lower grades.

Air Traffic Control Lanes

Obtain air traffic control maps from airlines. Ask students to draw the airline paths across the country (or world). Have them determine if there are shorter routes, and if so, why the airlines use the ones they do.

Battlefield

Make the bulletin board into a game grid for role playing war games. Students can make a gameboard familiar to them, or design their own. Vary the countries, terrain, weather, number of soldiers, etc.

City Subway

Find maps of subway (or bus) routes in cities around the world and post them on the bulletin board. Have students write chase scenes for each other through the subway system, changing subways and directions, searching for clues, treasures, or solving mysteries. (See the Great Maltese Circumglobal Trophy Dash, P.O. Box 53, LaCanada, CA 91011.)

Community Maps

Have students draw an enlarged map of the community and mark the locations of government offices—for example, licensing bureaus, accountants, courts, police stations, utility offices, social security office. This can be expanded throughout the year as students learn more about government.

Corporate Structures

After visiting corporations and interviewing personnel, students should construct corporate structure maps on the bulletin board, showing how information is communicated through the company and decisions are made. Have them compare their work with each other.

Food Distribution

Post a world map on the bulletin board. Ask students not only to locate food sources, but also to add transportation routes, and to research the problems of distributing food to the poor and to places of famine and war.

The History of Transportation

Post a U.S. or world map on the bulletin board. Have students research and illustrate historical methods of transportation around the world. Then they can add the drawings to the map in the correct locations.

The Mission Trail

Place a large map of California on the bulletin board. Have students research, illustrate, and list attributes of the Spanish missions in California. Then have them attach their work to the board.

Mystery Maps

Maps show unusual geographic features. Students can try to figure out *why* they are there or what caused certain events, as in solving a mystery.

Example 1: Place a map of Florida that shows Lake Okeechobee on the bulletin board. Have students hypothesize the presence and formation of the lake, giving only the facts.

Example 2: Study the disappearance of a town. Use two maps that show where a town has disappeared over time. Ask students to explain its disappearance (14).

Rivers

Post a state, U.S., or world map on the bulletin board. Let students color and label the rivers with dark blue markers. Ask students to list the geography of the area around each river; mark historical happenings on the rivers; and record the changes in population, ecology, and economics that have occurred over time.

World History Today

Post a large world map, or separate maps of the continents or countries, on the bulletin board. Have each student focus on one country during the year, and mark not only the historical happenings in that country, but current events from newspapers and magazines.

MATHEMATICS

K-3

Floor Maps

Ask students to measure the rooms in their house or their dream house and draw a floor plan to scale on a large posterboard. Advanced students can make a three-dimensional floor plan or architect's model of their house with foam board.

Math Mail

Place a figure of a mail carrier with a mailbag on the bulletin board and rows of numbered houses made from manila envelopes along a "street." The house numbers can be answers to math problems from the mailbag. Problems, written on envelopes as "letters," can be addition or subtraction; they can be changed as students learn more difficult math. Multiplication and division problems can be used for upper grades. Self-checking answers can be written on the letter flaps. *Note*: This activity can be added to the community bulletin board (15).

Multiplication Tables

The multiplication table grid is really a "map" teaching how to use coordinates, as well as multiplication. Draw a large grid on the bulletin board and let students make their own number flashcards. Students can practice their multiplication facts on the bulletin board.

Grades 4-8

Some of these bulletin board suggestions may be appropriate for advanced students in grades 1-3, or for slower learners in the upper grades.

Areas and Perimeters

Ask students to prepare large house plans for each other, with questions about carpeting and floor tiling, and fencing. Have them place their floor plans and questions on the bulletin board for other students to answer, measuring on the board.

Enlarging Patterns

The bulletin board can serve as the working space for enlarging designs from pattern books or magazines. Draw graph grids of several sizes with dark markers. Let students put their papers on top of the grids and, using the pattern book, enlarge their designs.

Exchange Rates

On a world map, ask students to list the currencies for each country and then to post the appropriate exchange rate as found in the daily newspaper. Students can write and calculate their own problems (19).

Geometry Geoboard

Put 81 pushpins two inches apart on the bulletin board to make a grid. Have students use yarn to form geometric shapes. Their instructions: "Make and name a polygon." They can identify the number of vertices and sides each shape has and enlarge shapes from books. This exercise can also be used to find areas, perimeters, and curves, and to locate points (15).

Graphing Quadrants

Place two lines intersecting each other on the bulletin board; label one "x" and the other "y." Label the quadrants I, II, III, IV. Lightly draw a grid. In an envelope, put cards with ordered pairs to find on the graph. Students can practice graphing skills by looking for the points on the graph.

History of Numbers

Post a world map on the bulletin board. Ask students to research and attach items about different number systems and their histories—for example, Arabic, Chinese, Roman.

Advanced: Students can chart the flow of money systems across countries and time. They can also mark the places where certain coins were found in archaeological digs.

Interest Rates:
Buying on Time Flowchart

Have students look in the newspaper or brochures of financial institutions for interest rates. Have them look in the classified ads to find prices for cars, vans, boats, houses. Ask them to flowchart the entire process of buying an item using standard flowcharting patterns.

For example: START. Find item you want in classified ads. Read the first ad. Do you like the item? (No. Read next ad. Loop.) Yes. Circle it in pen. Do you want to read more ads? (Yes. Read next ad. Loop.) No. Pick out the ad you want. Cut it out. Does ad have price? (No. Call telephone number in ad.) Yes. Write down price. Price = "P." Can you afford the price of the item now? Yes. STOP. No. Do you know interest rates for loans?

Metric Conversions

Post road maps on the bulletin board. Ask students to convert the miles listed to kilometers.

Scales of Miles

Post several maps of the same location with varying scales on the board. Ask students to compare the scales and figure out the distance between the same places on the different maps.

Sundials

Draw a large circle on the bulletin board to represent a sundial. Draw in the hours. Make shadows of different sizes, post them, and have students read the times.

Advanced. Students can figure the angles of the different times of day at different points on the earth (the scale varies with latitude). Correlate this exercise with any history lessons—for example, the pyramids, Stonehenge, Indian sun-watch poles.

Time Zones

Post a map of the United States or the world. Ask students to draw the time zones on the map and figure out the time in different locations. Have them write questions for each other about the zones, and plan trips, referring to airline time schedules.

Weather Maps

Post a map of the world on the bulletin board. Have students look in the newspaper for temperatures of cities around the world and put flags or small cards with readings in both centigrade and Fahrenheit for the locations, doing the necessary conversions.

63

Where Does Your Money Go?

Have students map where their money goes locally, nationally, and internationally. Post community, state, U.S., and world maps on the bulletin board. Ask students to put arrows with amounts or percentages (approximate) to the places they shop, to state government programs, and to federally financed programs.

Grades 9–12

Some of these bulletin board suggestions may be appropriate for advanced students in grades 6-8. Slower high school learners can also use boards suggested for the lower grades.

Air Traffic Lanes

Place air traffic lane maps on the bulletin board. Given wind speed and airplane speed, have students calculate the paths to various airports, showing how long it would take to fly from one to another, compensating for drift.

Geometric Shapes

Ask students to select an item and, using construction paper, make a geometric figure of it for the bulletin board. For example, at Halloween, they could make a geometric cat, being sure that all the pieces of paper they use are standard geometric shapes—parallelograms, trapezoids, triangles (equilateral, isosceles, right), parabolas, spheres, ellipses. Then ask other students to identify each shape. Suggestions might include the *Mayflower*, a Pilgrim boy or girl, a transformer robot (which transforms to something else like a car or a truck), a Christmas tree, an animal or a plant.

Hyperspace Calculations

This activity is similar to Air Traffic Lanes, but it uses solar system, galaxy, or science fiction space maps. Given the specifications of the orbit (mean distance, period, etc.) and the velocity and angle of travel, ask students to plot their courses. (See "Space Travel in Literature," p. 53.)

International Trade

Explore international banking and the import/export business on a world map. Have students research and mark on the map how a bank in Country A deals with a bank in Country B to buy raw materials from Country C to manufacture a product and sell it around the world.

Latitude and Longitude

Post an outline of a world map on the bulletin board. Ask students to interpolate the longitude and latitude of different points to the minute and second. (U.S. geological contour maps can also be used.)

Roads and Circles

Curving roads are parts of circles. Using geometry, and with a large protractor and compass, students can place on the bulletin board various degrees of curves (arcs) and find the dimensions of the circle they are a part of.

Rocketry

On one side of the bulletin board, label parts of the atmosphere from earth to space. Have students make paper rockets and add different velocities to them. Ask students to put up the rockets at different angles and figure out where each rocket will land (given the angle of initial velocity above the horizon).

Scatter Diagram

Place a large graph on the bulletin board. Have students plot ordered pairs from their researches (such as their height and weight) and construct a linear model, using yarn, to "average" the data. At first, students may estimate; then they should use the least-squares method ($m = ah + b$) to invent a polynomial to approximate the data (1).

Taking a "Pole" of the Class

Ask students to locate the position of their desks by measuring the distance and angle (polar coordinates) from a point on the floor with a given ray as the positive x-axis. On the bulletin board, draw a polar coordinate grid of circles. Have students put a small paper with their coordinates and initials in the appropriate graph location (1).

Your Initials in Parabolas

Have students make large letters of their initials from construction paper using parabolas. Have them also write an equation for each parabola with the appropriate domain. (For example, the letter ''A'' can be made with the parabola equations of $y = -x^2 + 9$ and $y = x^2$) (1). Then students can put the letters on the bulletin board. 100

SCIENCE

K-3

Dinosaur Habitats

As students study dinosaurs, have them draw the different climates and vegetation forms of the Mesozoic Era on a large blank world map. Show them how to make and use a key, legend, and map symbols for different map features. They can cut out their pictures of dinosaurs and place them in the correct habitat.

Life Cycle of Animals

Put up a background that will reflect the color of the habitat of the animals the class is studying. Have students draw pictures of the different stages in an animal's life cycle and put them up in a circular or sequential configuration, showing the change of habitat (e.g., for a frog) as the animal moves through different stages (4).

Solar System

Have students make a map of the solar system to scale (math skills) on the bulletin board, using their creativity in choosing materials. Or, have them make a three-dimensional solar system ''map'' across the entire room, with papier-mâché ''planets'' hanging from the ceiling.

Space Exploration

Mark off one side of the bulletin board with the distances between the earth's surface and space. Have students learn and label the various atmospheric levels, draw rocket ships, and place them in various levels. If desired, have children research historical rocket types and put them in the highest altitude they traveled. Let students be as detailed as they wish in their drawings. Add rockets and satellites from other countries. If a rocket launch is in progress, follow its progress each day on a world map.

Weather Maps

Laminate (or cover with clear adhesive plastic) a world or U.S. map. Using newspaper weather maps and television weather reports, use water soluble markers to demonstrate cold fronts, warm fronts, highs, lows, etc., on the classroom map. Then have students give the weather report each day, marking the symbols on the map, and erasing them the next day for another student.

Grades 4–8

Some of these bulletin boards may be appropriate for advanced students in grades 1-3, or for slower learners in the upper grades.

Atoms

Draw a small circle (about 3 inches in diameter) in the center of the bulletin board. This represents the nucleus of an atom. Around it, draw concentric circles representing the atomic shells. Cut out approximately 30 small circles of three different colors to represent electrons, protons, and neutrons. Put these in three envelopes attached to the board. In another envelope, place large cards with the periodic table information for each element: atomic number, mass, symbol, and electronic configuration. Have students pick a large card and put the correct number of small circles—electrons, protons, and neutrons—in the nucleus and the orbits.

Biomes of Life

Ask students to draw or find pictures of the main ecological biomes (desert, rain forest, jungle, grassland) and place them around a world map. They can stretch yarn between the biome and the area it covers on the map.

Body Maps

Draw an outline of a human body on the bulletin board background paper. Ask students to research and draw the paths of blood and air through the body, labeling body parts and the flow of O_2 and CO_2.

Constellations

Place a dark blue or black background paper on the bulletin board. Have students study different constellations and then map them on the bulletin board, figuring out where they would be in relation to others. This might also be done on the ceiling, using reflective paper cut into stars.

Contour Mapping

Post a U.S. geological contour map on the bulletin board and cover it with acetate. Ask students to mark ridges and drainage basins to locate the watershed areas.

Earthquakes

On a world map, keep track of the earthquakes that take place around the world. This will automatically map the major faults.

Glaciers

As students study glaciers, have them plot glaciers and their movements today, as well as in past glacial periods, on a world map.

Light Bulbs

Draw different configurations of light bulbs and wires on the bulletin board. Ask students to trace the flow of electricity and figure out what happens to the different light bulbs when one is off and another is on. Real wires and light bulbs attached to the board can also be used for this activity.

Microscope

Place a large cross section of a microscope on the bulletin board. Have students trace a light ray through the system.

Rain Forests

Rain forest ecology, so important to learn about as these forests dwindle, can be taught while plotting the rain forest areas on a world map. Have students note their decline, and draw a cross-section of a rain forest, showing where the animal populations live.

Ring of Fire

Track the volcanoes that have erupted throughout history. This will locate the Ring of Fire for students. Compare with "Earthquakes."

State Geology

On a blank state map, ask students to plot mountains, lakes, rivers, moraines, deltas, etc. Have them use standard mapping symbols or make up their own.

The U.S.A. at Night

On dark blue paper, draw an outline map of the United States. Ask students to look up the populations of cities of various sizes across the country. Assign several students to each city. Use yellow paper dots to indicate population. First, decide the number of people each dot represents—1,000 or 5,000, for example. Then, have students determine the number of dots needed for each city and place them on the map in the appropriate location.

Volcanoes

A cross section of a volcano is a map. Draw or make a sectional diagram of a volcano out of paper. Have students label it.

Water Cycle

Have students draw lakes, rivers, or oceans and flat, rolling, and mountainous land. Ask them to add arrows and labels for evaporation, condensation, transpiration, respiration, etc., and clouds, plants, and animals as desired.

Grades 9—12

Some of these bulletin boards may be appropriate for advanced students in grades 6-8. Slower high school learners can also use boards suggested for the lower grades.

Animal Migration

Attach a large world map to the bulletin board. Have students cut out large arrows to indicate animal migration and place them on the map, labeling them with the name of the animal.

Atomic Energy:
Production and Disposal

Post a world map on the bulletin board. Ask students to research, locate, and mark the locations of atomic energy plants, the amount of energy they produce, and the places where the nuclear waste is buried.

Bending Light

Draw diagrams of convex and concave mirrors on large posters and laminate them. Post them on either side of the bulletin board. Ask students to calculate the angles of reflection given the different angles of incidence. This activity may also be used for the refraction of lenses using Snell's Law.

Chromosome Mapping

Draw the human chromosome configuration on the bulletin board. As students learn about different genes, they can plot them on the chromosomes and label them.

Circuits of Technology

1. Post a large diagram of the circuit board of a computer. Ask students to figure it out.
2. Have students trace the flow of information through a com-

puter system, showing keyboard, monitor, disk drive, programs, files, etc.

3. Draw a large circle on the bulletin board. Ask students to map a diskette, showing how information is stored.

DNA-RNA Flannelgraph

Cover the bulletin board with flannel. Cut out a large cell shape of flannel and add it to the board. Cut out smaller shapes of felt or flannel (or paper backed with sandpaper) in the forms of the amino acid (standard) code that shows how DNA and RNA replicate and transfer information. Show students how to move the felt pieces around, in and out of the cell, how the loose amino acids "floating" in the cells hook up to replicate the DNA, and how messenger and transfer RNA work. Let students practice using the code and checking each other's knowledge.

Electric Fields

Place a piece of acetate on the bulletin board and ask students to sketch field lines around different arrangements of plus (+) and (–) charges. Students calculate the interactions of the fields, which depend upon the squares of the distances. This activity may also be done for magnetic fields.

Electricity

On a house floor plan posted on the bulletin board, ask students to place yarn, thin wire, or string to show possible electrical circuitry. Let others analyze this and change it as they wish.

Hit It!

Place pictures of two inanimate objects (e.g., automobiles) on the bulletin board, facing each other. Move them together until they hit each other (one may remain stationary). Given the initial velocities and masses of the two objects, ask students to calculate final velocities and where both would end up.

Land Navigation

Post topographical maps on the bulletin board. Have students

71

use compasses to plan a hike. This is a good exercise before going into the field.

Parts of a Beach

When students visit a beach, ask them to take pictures of its striations or strata. Place the pictures on the bulletin board in order, labeling each section and telling how each was formed and what kinds of life may be found there. Compare the local beach structure with textbook diagrams, including comparisons on the bulletin board, if desired.

Periodic Table

The Periodic Table of Elements is a map, organized by the similarities and differences of elements.

1. Ask students to create a different configuration of the chart that still indicates the characteristics.

2. Draw an "empty" periodic table and have students make cards with the atomic information to fit each grid square. Have students fill up the grid; then take the cards down, shuffle them, and replace them in the correct order.

3. Post several examples of periodic charts and ask students to compare the different arrangements.

Photography Flowchart

Have students make a flowchart of the steps necessary to develop and print film. Ask them to include the chemicals and the reactions. Place examples of each step on the bulletin board (i.e., include underexposed and overexposed pictures).

Rocks—Where Are They?

On a local, state, U.S., or world map, have students label the places where different kinds of rocks are found—for example, slate, granite, quartz, and sandstone, as well as such types as sedimentary, igneous, and metamorphic rock.

Roller Coasters

Have students make a roller-coaster track on the bulletin board, with paper cars of different masses and velocities. Ask students to calculate whether or not the cars will fall off the hills and curves.

Tectonic Plates

Place a world map on the bulletin board. Use a map of the sea floor, if desired. Have students research and plot the locations of the earth's tectonic plates. Have them label the amount of movement per year, and show past movement with plastic overlays.

Tidepool Life

Cut out a large blue or green paper circle and place it on the bulletin board. Surround it with "rocks" cut out of paper. As the class studies tidepool life, have students draw or cut pictures from magazines of the animal and plant life and put them into the tidepool. Add labels and characteristics of specimens as desired.

Tides

Students can (1) mark major tides in the world; (2) note on their beach map (see "Parts of a Beach," p. 72) the location of high and low tide levels (correlated with a tide timetable and including times of day); (3) diagram the relationship of the earth and the moon and tides; and (4) chart waves.

Where Are the Elements?

On a world map, ask students to indicate where the chemical elements are found. Ask them to add the mining operations in each country, including capital investments.

For social studies, students can research and report on the economic and political implications of the locations of certain elements.

Will It Move?

Ask students to draw pictures of objects of different masses. Have them choose and describe a force to move each object. Given the coefficient of friction, students can calculate where the object will move and how fast. They can demonstrate their calculations on the bulletin board.

OTHER ACTIVITIES

K-3

Child Development Time Line

Draw a line along the top of the bulletin board, measuring 72 equal distance segments. Label from 0 months to 6 years (or however long you want to go.) Using baby pictures of students' family members or from magazines, ask students to place the pictures on the time line at the correct age. Discuss the differences. More advanced students can describe the differences in writing.

As a followup, bring babies of different ages into the classroom so that students can see how they match the pictures. For younger students, the teacher can write down the characteristics they observe on a language experience chart.

Note: Although this activity was used in a K-3 class, it can be used at any level, even in high school home economics classes.

Orchestra/Band Seating
(Music)

Draw concentric semicircles on the bulletin board. Ask students to draw pictures of musical instruments on cards and place them for orchestral (or band) seating. Visit a symphony orchestra to see how the instruments are arranged. Discuss possible differences and the reason for them.

Table Setting
(Home Economics)

Draw a large rectangle or a circle on the bulletin board to represent a table. Younger students can cut out paper dishes and utensils and place them in the correct places. Older students can calculate the amount of space to allow per person and the number of people per table according to the size of each place setting.

Grades 4-8

The Book Company
(Economics)

After a class has bound its own writings, students can organize a

74

corporation to mass produce and sell the books. The bulletin board can be a flowchart of activities: studying other corporations; printing and distributing shares; electing officers; deciding upon content, illustrations, and binding; assembling the books; printing; advertising; selling; etc. This activity was originally planned for grades 4-6 (5).

Clothing and Design
(Home Economics)

Post a world map on the bulletin board. Ask students to collect samples of fabric from different parts of the world and attach them to the appropriate places. They can also find pictures of different styles and costumes from different countries and periods of history and add these to the board. In addition, they can research the origins of fabrics and styles as well as their influence on today's designs.

Design and Layout
(Art)

Ask students to read books on design, the use of color, and the principles of layout, and then experiment on the bulletin board with shapes and colors.

Drug Map
(Drug Education)

On the bulletin board, have students develop a sequential map of drug use, from first use to death, showing side effects, behavior changes, etc. This activity can also be used for alcoholism.

Music in Time and Space
(Music)

Place a map of the world on the bulletin board. After they have read about different cultures, ask students to draw something that represents a culture's musical heritage and place it on the board. Have them also include historical information.

For advanced students, add cultural variation in tonal systems by jotting down the scales and chants on a staff (12).

Sports from Other Countries
(Physical Education)

On a world map, ask students to add flashcards and pictures of sports to their countries of origin. For example,

Polo – England
Soccer – Europe, South America
Rugby – England
Bullfighting – Spain, Mexico
Jai alai – Mexico, Cuba (7)

Typewriter Keys
(Typing)

Draw a blank grid of a typewriter keyboard on the bulletin board. Make flashcards of all the characters and put them in an envelope attached to the board. Ask students to find the keys for all the cards, without referring to an actual typewriter.

Code Game. Ask students to write sentences as if their fingers were on the wrong typewriter keys. Then, ask other students to crack the code.

Where Are Those Songs?
(Music)

On a world map, ask students to find the places that the composers of band and orchestral pieces wrote about—for example, the steppes of Central Asia, the Moldau, the fountains of Rome, a night in the tropics, Appalachian spring, Chattanooga choo-choo (12).

Grades 9–12

Blocking
(Drama)

Draw an outline of a stage on the bulletin board. Make characters out of paper and symbols for scenery. Have student directors try various blocking strategies to learn how to best move cast members around.

Careers
(Career Education)

Use a flowchart, a diagram, or a storyboard to show the elements of career education. Start with high school, then branch to college, vocational education, and on-the-job training. Show the importance of certain subjects in various careers, expanding the map into the possible jobs for each student's area of interest.

Circles of Influence
(Sociology)

Ask students to map the personal relationships within a group of people (perhaps the class—but be careful about possible hurt feelings). Include extended family, neighborhoods, country leadership.

Community Businesses
(Marketing)

Post a community map on the bulletin board. Ask students to locate and mark all the businesses in the area. Then, ask them to decide what new business could prosper, where it should go, and why.

Football
(Physical Education)

Draw an area on the bulletin board to represent the football field. With paper dots denoting players, have students plan tactics together. Leave a new plan on the board for constant review.

The Homeless
(Sociology)

Post a world map on the bulletin board. Ask students to find out where homeless people, including refugees, live, where they come from, and trace their routes. Have them add the reasons why people become homeless.

Marching Band Formations
(Music)

Outline the area for the football field on the bulletin board.

Make paper dots for each musician or group of musicians. Have students study band formations as they move players (dots) around on the field.

Newspaper Galleys
(Journalism)

Plan student newspaper page layouts using a bulletin board like a pasteup sheet. Move stories around until they fit, discussing pros and cons of placement.

Shopping Malls
(Marketing)

Draw the floor plan of a local shopping mall. Ask students to plan to start a new business (such as a child-care center), determine its potential in the mall, as well as where it should go and why.

Store Layouts
(Marketing)

Draw an outline map of a store, empty of merchandise, but including the aisles and fixtures. Ask students to draw small pictures (or make labels) of merchandise and arrange them in the store, planning where each type of item should go and why.

What If . . . ?
(International Accounting)

Place a large world map on the bulletin board and an enlarged profit/loss statement at the side. Ask students to make up their own case studies, using flashcards with the numbers involved, exchanging and moving them as they figure their profit and loss decisions. Using the newspaper for current exchange rates, ask students to answer the questions: "Shall we exchange the currency at the time of the business transaction or later?" and "Shall we exchange currency in different countries at the same/different times?" The figures on the profit/loss statement will change with the answers to these questions and students can use the bulletin board to calculate them.

BIBLIOGRAPHY

1. Allinger, Glenn D. "The 10-Minute Mathematics Bulletin Board." *Mathematics Teacher* 76, no. 6 (September 1983): 400–406.
2. Anderson, Jeremy. "Self-Guided Walking Tours to Teach Orientation." *Journal of Geography* 85 (November-December 1986): 271.
3. Ballard, Robert D. "A Long Last Look at *Titanic.*" *National Geographic* (December 1986): 698–727.
4. *Brain-Buster Bulletin Boards.* New York: Instructor Publications, 1984.
5. Brouwer, Elaine. *The Book Company.* Middleburg Heights, Ohio: Signal Publishing, 1982.
6. Bruno, Angela. "Hands-On Wins Hands-Down." *Early Years* 13, no. 2 (October 1982): 60–67.
7. Burke, Kenneth, and Kranhold, Julie. *Ideas for Sports.* Belmont, Calif.: Fearon Publications, 1973, p. 16.
8. Collingford, Cedric. "Wall Displays—Children's Reactions." *Education 3-13* (October 1978): 12–14.
9. Creekmore, W. N. "Effective Use of Classroom Walls." *Academic Therapy* (March 1987): 341–48. EJ 350 896.
10. Cunningham, Glenn. "Ten Questions That Shook the Class." *Phi Delta Kappa* (October 1986): 158–60.
11. Davies, B. G. "Displaying Mathematics." *Mathematics in School* 16, no. 2 (March 1987): 33–35.
12. Demko, George J. "Ideas on How to Enliven the Teaching of Geography." *Journal of Geography* (November-December 1986): 246–48.
13. Dunn, Rita. "Now That You Know Your Learning Style, How Can You Make the Most of It?" *Early Years* 13, no. 6 (February 1983): 59–64.
14. Felton, Randall, and Allen, Rodney F. "Using Mysteries to Teach Geography and Questioning Skills." *Journal of Geography* 86 (January-February 1987): 32–33.
15. Gersting, Judith, and others. "Banish the Boring Bulletin Board." *Arithmetic Teacher* 25, no. 4 (January 1978): 44–46.
16. Gomez, Linda. "Eight Great Buried Treasures." *Life* (March 1987): 29–38.
17. Guthrie, John T. "Story Comprehension." *Reading Teacher* 30, no. 5 (February 1977): 574–76.
18. Haas, Mary E. "Geography and the Active Learning Bulletin Board." *Journal of Geography* 86 (March-April 1987): 76–77.

19. Kirman, Joseph M. "Integrating Geography with Other School Subjects." *Journal of Geography* 87, no. 3 (May-June 1988): 104-5.
20. Laurain, Lucy L. *Display*. Stevensville, Mich.: Educational Service, 1975.
21. Leslie, Connie. "Lost on Planet Earth." *Newsweek*, August 8, 1988; p. 31.
22. McCarthy, Bernice. *The 4MAT* System. Oakbrook, Ill.: Excel, 1980.
23. McPhie, Walter E. "The Bulletin Board: Let It Tell Your Story." *Clearing House* 52, no. 8 (April 1979): 359–61.
24. Pittelman, Susan D.; Levin, Kathy M.; and Johnson, Dale D. "A Semantic Mapping Lesson Plan." *Reading Teacher* 40, no. 2 (November 1986): 236–38.
25. Prizzi, Elaine, and Hoffman, Jeanne. *Teaching Off the Wall*. Belmont, Calif.: Pitman Learning, 1981.
26. Rees, Alun L. W. "The Display Board in Language Teaching." *TESOL Quarterly* 4, no. 2 (June 1970): 161–64.
27. Reseigh, Donna J. "Bulletin Boards That Get Students Involved." *Foreign Language Annals* 10, no. 3 (May 1977): 281–83.
28. Schafer, Larry E. "Bulletin Boards as an Instructional Art." *Science and Children* 19, no. 2 (October 1981): 32–34.
29. Stewart, E. D. "Learning Styles Among Gifted/Talented Students: Preferences for Instructional Techniques." Doctoral dissertation, University of Connecticut, 1979.
30. Swabb, Barbara Sloan. *Mathematics Bulletin Boards*. Belmont, Calif.: Pitman Learning, 1971.
31. Thorpe, Janet M. "Bulletin Boards for Ostriches." *Elementary English* 66, no. 7 (November 1969): 959–62.
32. Wasson, F. R. "A Comparative Analysis of Learning Styles and Personality Characteristics of Achieving and Underachieving Gifted Elementary Students." Doctoral dissertation, Florida State University, 1980.